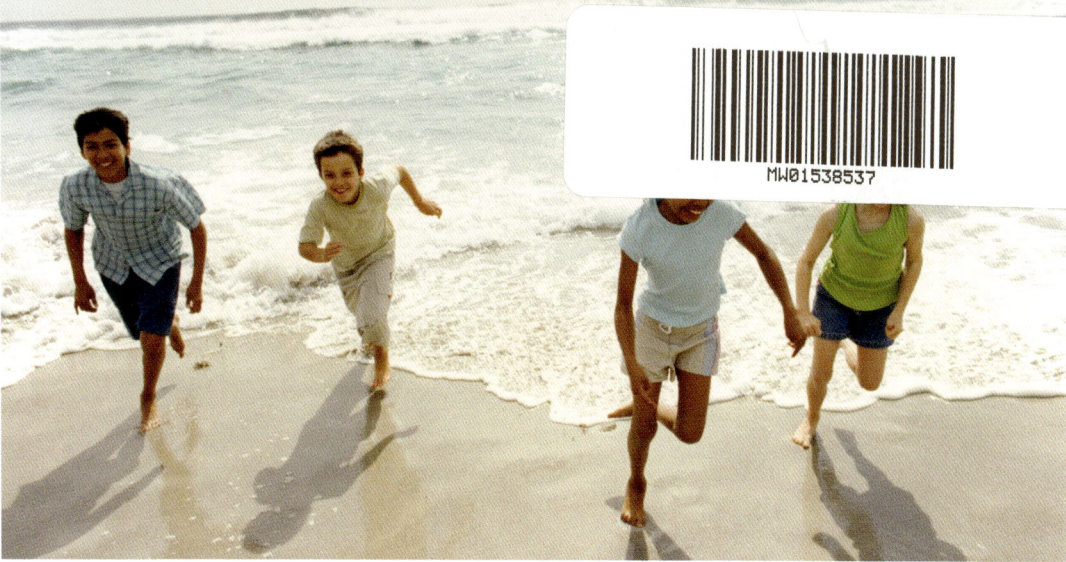

Your Heart

by Lola M. Schaefer

Table of Contents

What and Where Is Your Heart? 2

What Does Your Heart Do?. 6

What Is Your Heartbeat and Pulse? 9

What Can Change Your Heart Rate? 14

How Can You Take Care of Your Heart?. 16

Glossary and Index .20

What and Where Is Your Heart?

Your **heart** is a **muscle**. The heart is one of the most important muscles in your body.

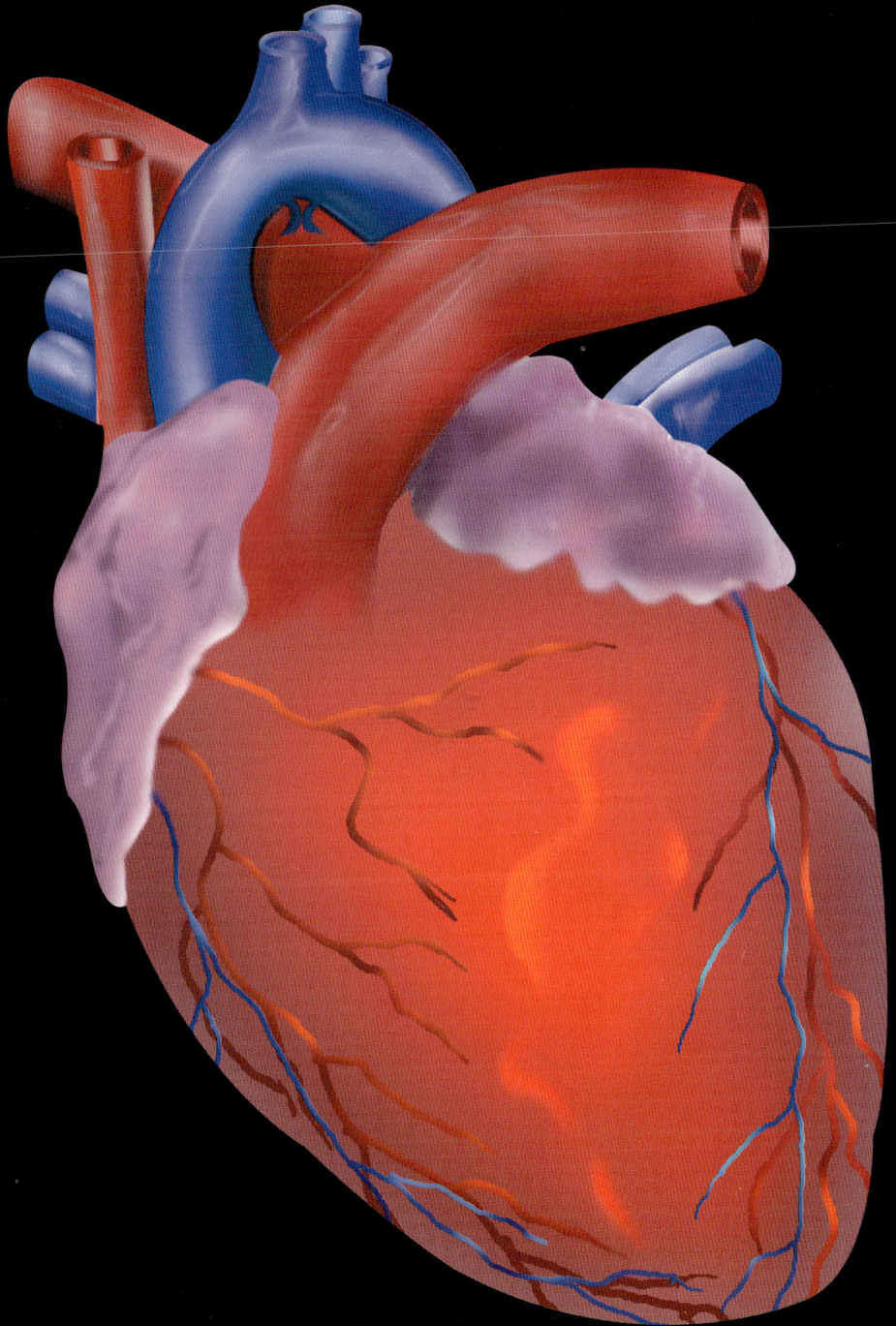

3

Your heart is in the middle of your body. It is inside your chest.

Your heart is between your two **lungs**.

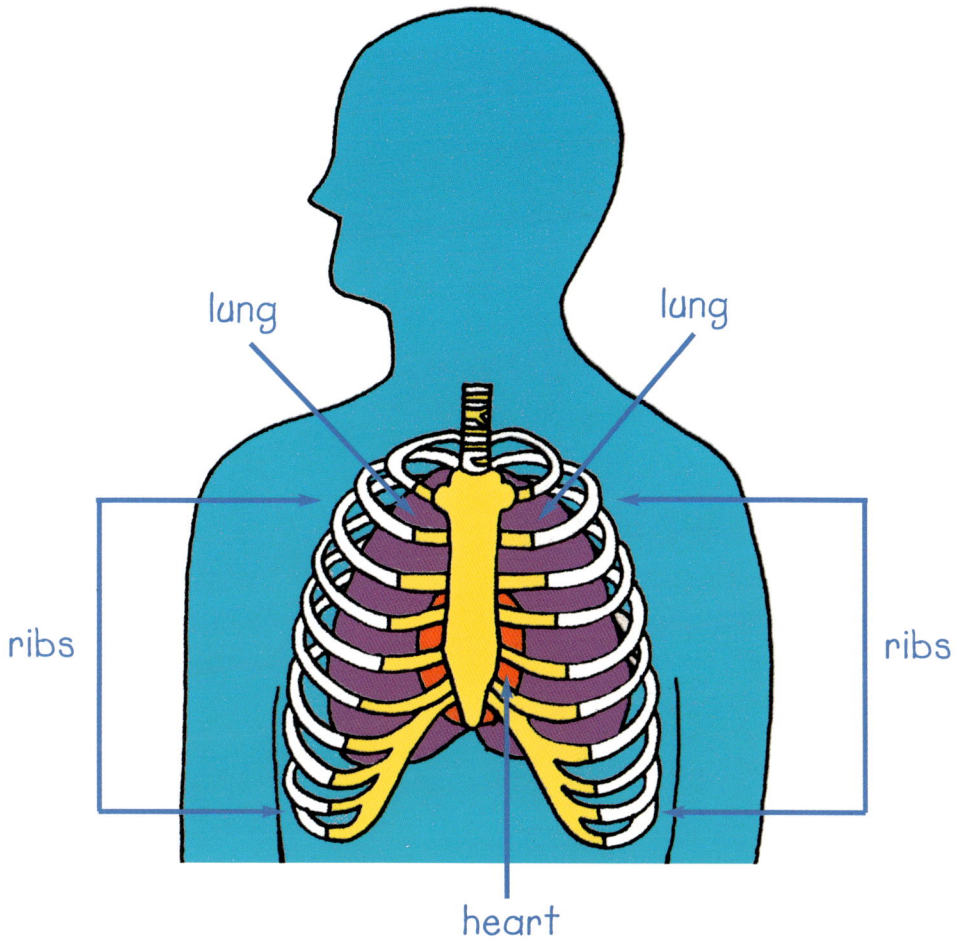

lung

lung

ribs

ribs

heart

Ribs are bones. They protect your heart in your chest.

What Does Your Heart Do?

Your heart **pumps blood**.

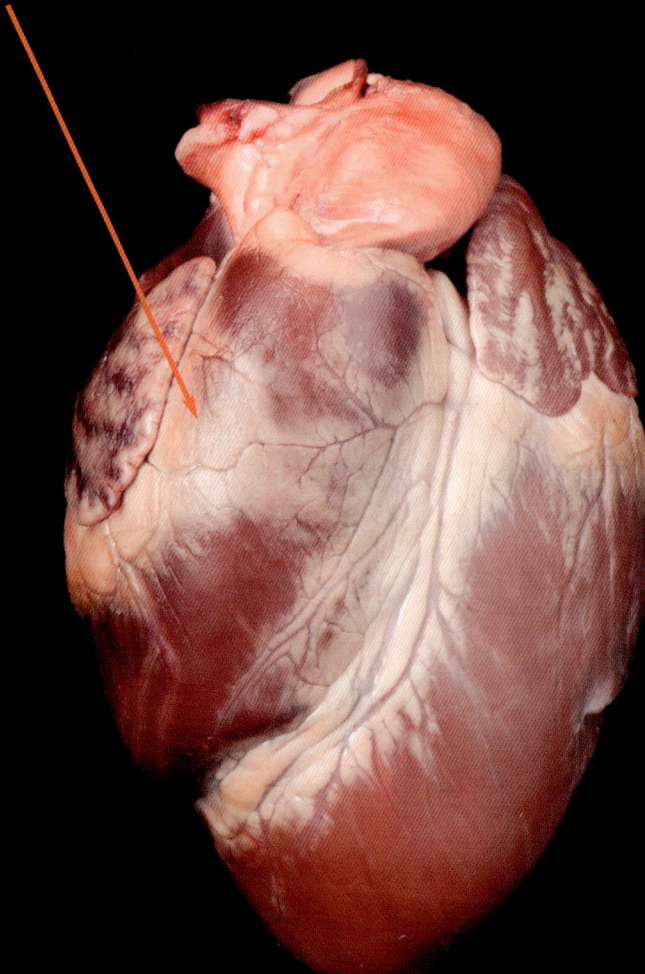

heart

Your body has many small tubes that carry the blood. Each time your heart pumps, it pushes blood through these tubes. These tubes carry the blood to every part of your body.

veins

arteries

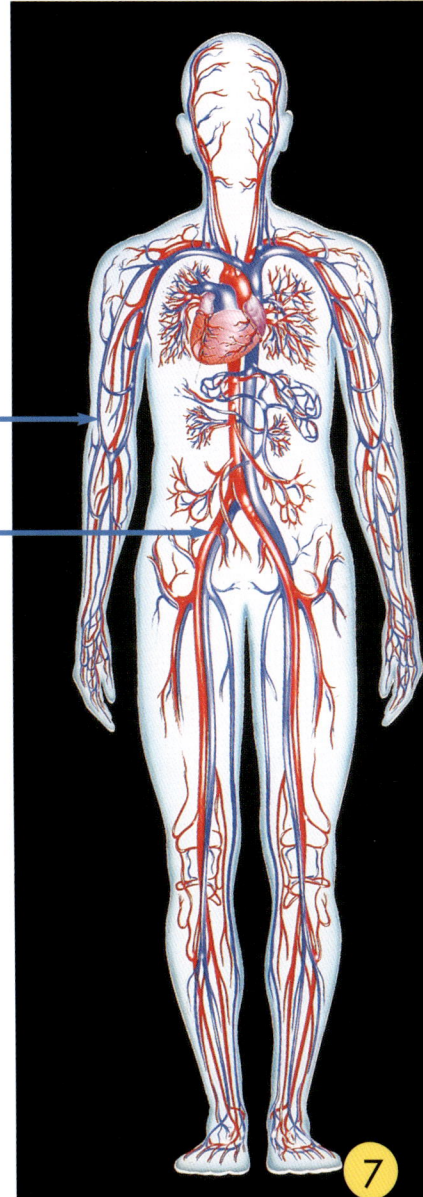

The tubes that carry your blood are called **arteries**, **veins**, and **capillaries**. The capillaries are too small to see in this drawing.

7

Your blood gets **oxygen** from the lungs and takes this oxygen back to the heart. Then your heart pumps this blood through your body.

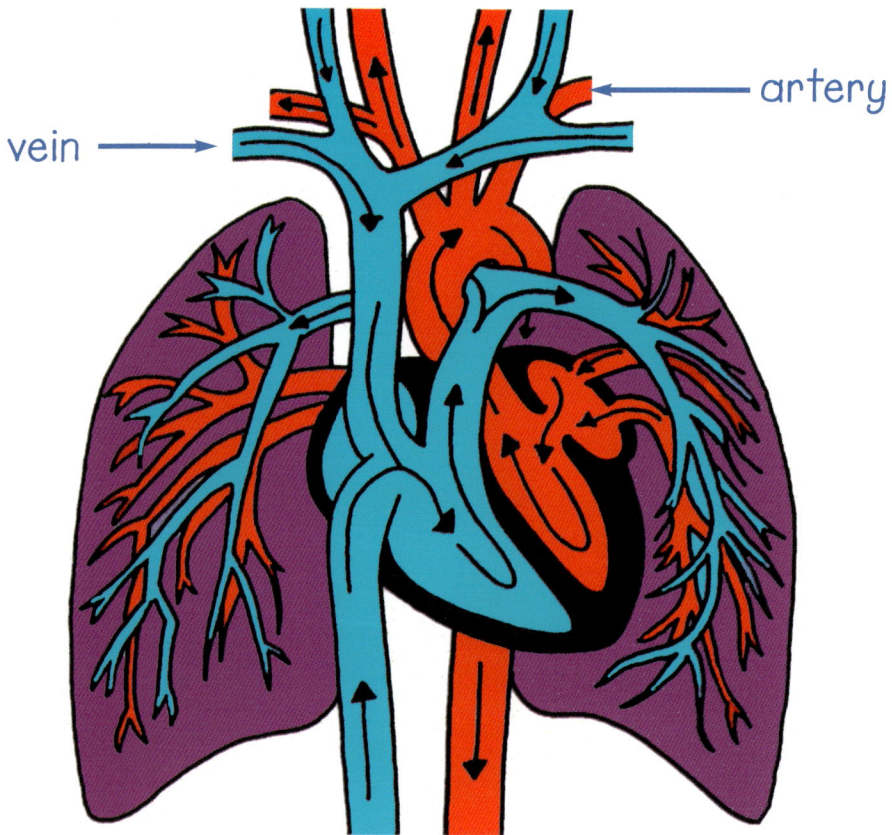

vein →

← artery

The red tubes are arteries that carry blood away from the heart. The blue tubes are veins that carry blood back to the heart.

What Is Your Heartbeat and Pulse?

Each time your heart pumps,
you can hear it. This is your **heartbeat**.
The doctor is listening
to this girl's heartbeat.

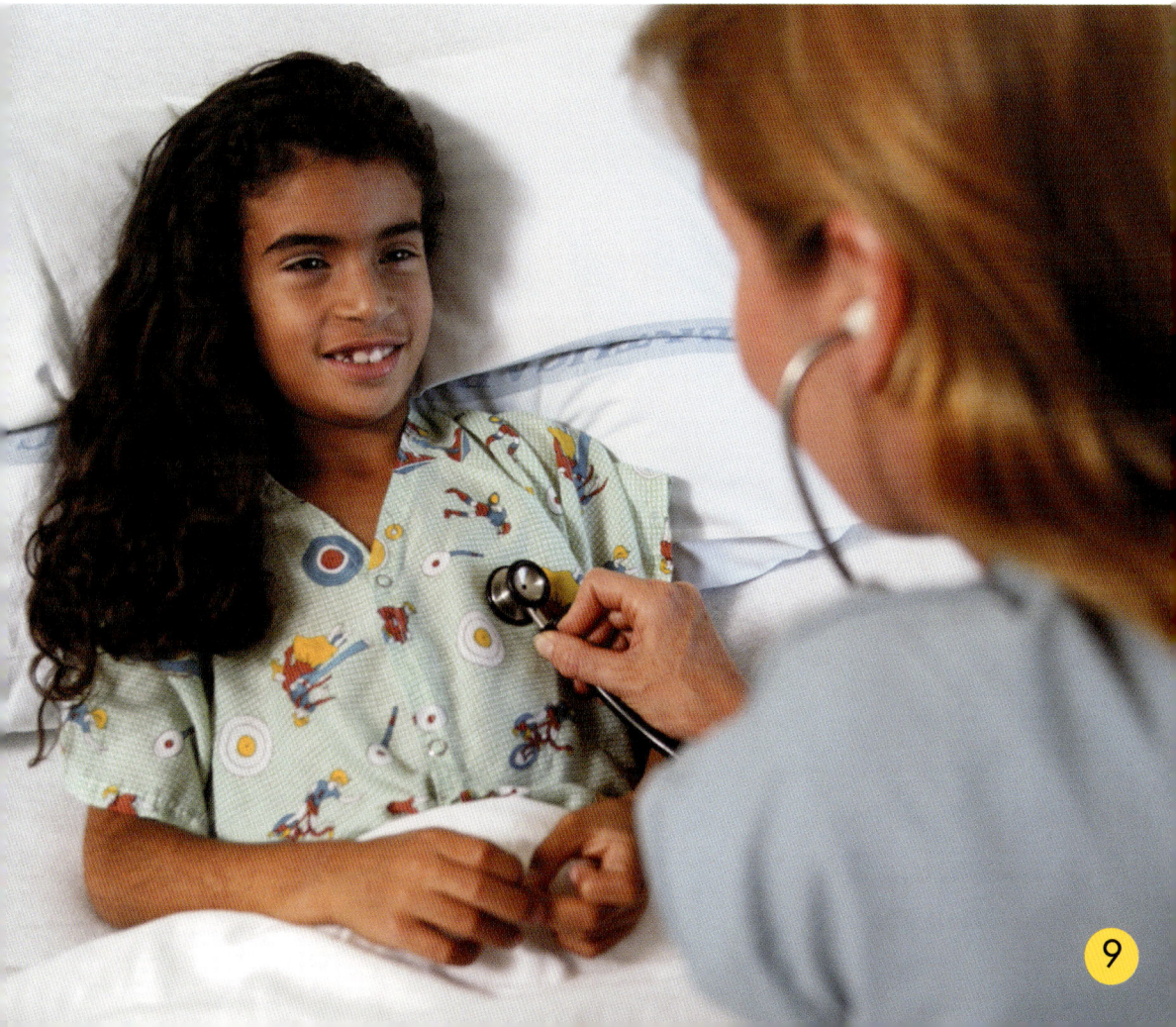

Your heart beats about seventy to ninety times each minute. This is called your **heart rate**. Small animals have high heart rates. Large animals have low heart rates.

mouse: 500 beats per minute   **elephant:** 28 beats per minute

The size of the animal determines how fast or slow the heart rate is.

Each heartbeat sends a push of blood through the tubes in your body. This push of blood can be felt. It is called your **pulse**.

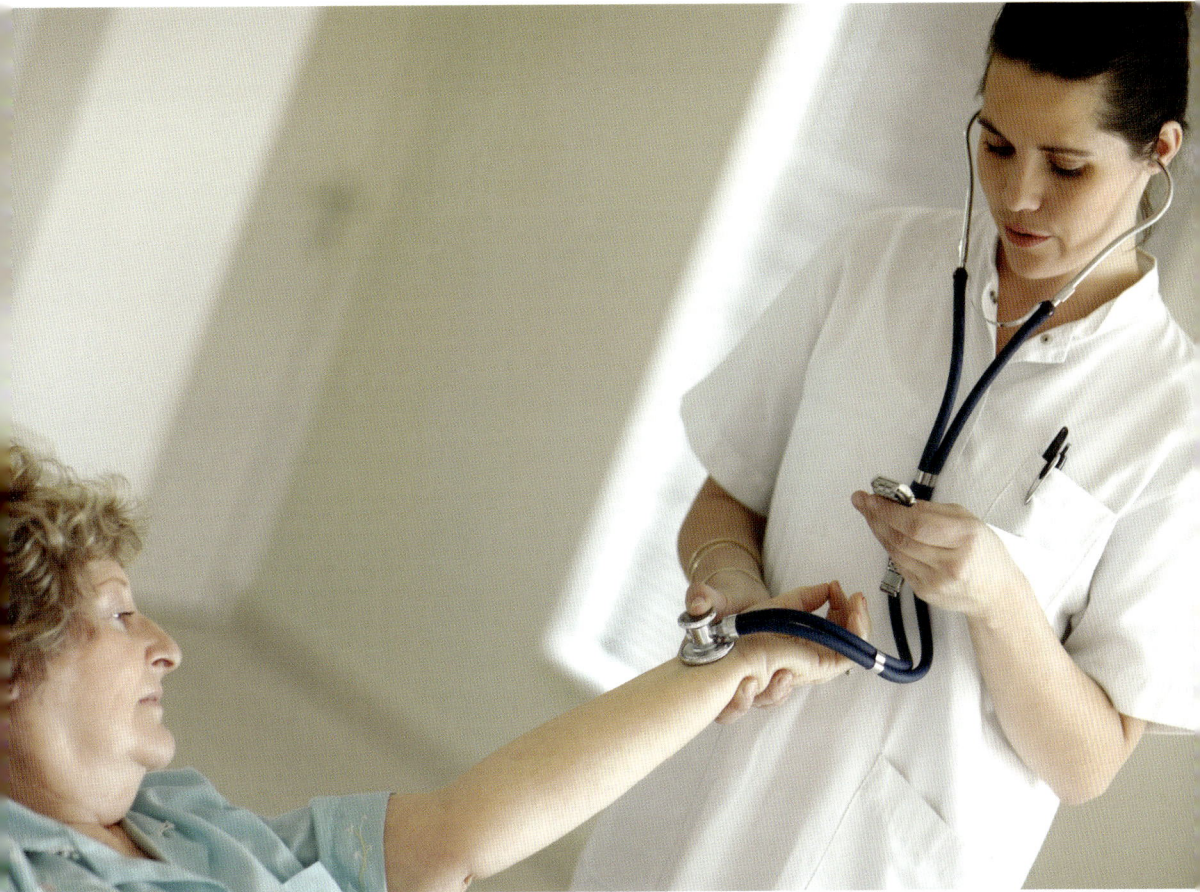

Nurses are trained to measure people's heart rates by counting the pulses.

You can measure your own heart rate.
Put two fingers on your neck
under your chin. Find a place
where you can feel your pulse.

Look at a clock. Count the number
of pulses you feel in one minute.
The number of pulses you feel
in one minute is your heart rate.

What Can Change Your Heart Rate?

Exercise makes the heart work harder.
Your heart rate is faster
right after you exercise.

When you exercise, your body
needs more oxygen from the blood.

Compare Heart Rates

name	heart rate before exercising	heart rate after exercising
Dan	84 pulses per minute	118 pulses per minute
Sue	86 pulses per minute	120 pulses per minute

Work with a partner to compare your heart rate before and after you do jumping jacks for one minute.

How Can You Take Care of Your Heart?

Exercise keeps your heart strong.
Like all muscles, it needs a good **workout**.
Walking, running, and jumping
are good exercises for the heart.

Eating good food helps keep your heart strong. Foods with too much salt or fat can hurt your heart.

Here are some examples of healthy foods for your heart and the rest of your body.

Do you want to know how hard your heart muscle works?

Try this. Hold a tennis ball in your hand. Squeeze the ball forty times. Is your hand tired?

Your heart muscle pumps blood all day and all night, every day of your life. But it never gets tired. Take good care of your heart and it will take good care of you!

Glossary

arteries (AR-ter-eez): tubes that carry blood from the heart to the rest of the body

blood (BLUD): the liquid made of tiny cells that the heart pumps through the body

capillaries (KA-pih-lair-eez): the smallest tubes that carry blood

exercise (EK-ser-size): an activity that helps your body stay healthy, like walking, running, or swimming

heart (HART): the muscle that pumps blood through the body

heartbeat (HART-beet): one complete pump of the heart

heart rate (HART RATE): the number of heartbeats in one minute

lungs (LUNGZ): the two organs for breathing located in the chest

muscle (MUH-sul): a body tissue that tightens to make body parts move

oxygen (AHK-sih-jen): a gas in the air that the human body needs

pulse (PULS): the push of blood that can be felt at certain points of the body

pumps (PUMPS): pushes blood through the body

ribs (RIBZ): the bones around the chest

veins (VANEZ): the tubes that carry blood back to the heart

workout (WERK-owt): exercise

Index

arteries 7, 8
blood 6, 7, 8, 11, 14, 19
capillaries 7
exercise 14
heartbeat 9, 11
heart rate 10–15
lungs 5, 8

muscle 2, 16, 18, 19,
oxygen 8, 14
pulse 11–13
pumps 6–9, 19
ribs 5
veins 7, 8
workout 16